Who Cut The Cheese?

A Parable of Personal Responsibility

by Molleen Zwiker Zanger

illustrated by Kurt Freidinger

This book is dedicated to the students
of English Composition 112
Section 63
Winter 2004
Delta College
University Center MI
who dared me, so it's all their fault!

David Allen
Douglas Bishop
Brett Brownlee
Julie Deska
Julie Ewald
Steven Foulds
Kathryn Gwizdala
Tracy Hagar
Thomas Johnson
Joel Katzenberger
Charles Krause
Zachary McKenna
Melissa Nowak
Kent Shick
Adam Simmons
Diantha Soares
Nicole Stanton
Blake Stapleton
Joel Taschner
Shaun Whitney
Amanda Zielinski

Who Cut the Cheese?

Early one gray, overcast Monday morning (of course it *had* to be
a Monday) four professionals were headed for work.

All four worked on the seventh floor of the Lemming Building right

downtown in the Renaissance Zone (you know the one – with the

gargoyles on the

ledges of

the roof).

The four professionals were named Eenie, Meenie, Minee, and Moe.

Co-incidentally, they all worked at the same firm, Flatt & U'Lance, so

they knew each other, at least by name.

As it happened, they all arrived at the elevator at the same time. If you remember from your fifth grade tour of the Lemming building, there are three elevators in the marble-clad entry. They are beautiful examples of the ornate style of the past, but

at any given moment,

one will be stuck between

the third and fourth

floors (many people say

the ghost of old man

Lemming jams it so he

can have a little quality

time with the ghost of his

secretary Muriel). The

other elevator will

invariably be

out of order.

So Eenie, Meenie, Minee, and Moe all stepped into the functioning

elevator and greeted each other as Eenie pulled back the big brass

handle that closed the collapsible gate and pushed the button for the

eighth floor. If you remember, that is the only way to get to the

seventh floor of the Lemming building – go to the eighth floor, then

back down to the seventh.

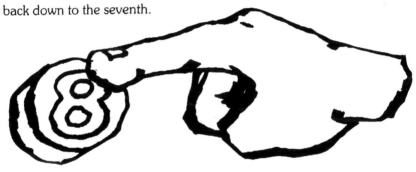

The elevator lurched

into its leisurely

ascent.

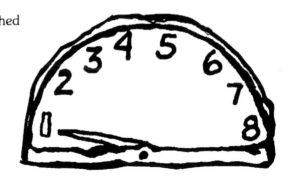

4

"Morning, Eenie," said Minee to Eenie. Then, "Morning Meenie.

Hey. Moe."

The elevator clanged and shook.

"Morning Minee," said Meenie. "Morning, Eenie. Morning Moe."

The elevator jolted the four slightly as it lumbered slowly upward.

"Morning, Meenie," said Moe, "Morning, Eenie. Morning, Minee."

Each smiled his best Oh-Shit-It's-Monday-Morning smile and

assumed his best feet-slightly-apart-both-hands-on-his-briefcase-

going-up-in-the-elevator stance and kept his face trained studiously

at the door, each silently willing the doors to open when they were

supposed to.

5

Eenie pursed his lips, about to start the silent whistle he unknowingly but habitually whistled when he had to wait for anything (like beautiful but slow and unreliable antique elevators)(or lines with over four people ahead of him at Ye Newe Deli which you may remember from the sixth grade class tour), when suddenly the unthinkable happened. You know what I mean, the thing we all secretly fear in an old, rickety elevator in an old, rickety building that any sane planning committee would have condemned instead of marking for "restoration" using an obscene amount of federal grant monies to slap on a coat of paint –

That's right – a distinctly disgusting odor faintly but surely began to fill the air.

Each professional first squinted his eyes as people often do when they can't believe their noses.

Then the odor got slightly stronger and slightly nastier

Each professional then surreptitiously shifted his eyes from left to right, expecting one of the others to be looking at the ceiling in the studied nonchalance of the caught-in-the-act guilty.

Then the odor got even stronger and decidedly noxious. There was no mistaking that odor: Someone had let loose one dandy booty clap. Someone had broken bad, bad wind. Someone had tooted a rip-roarer of an air biscuit, a butt belch. Someone was running silent but deadly. Someone had stepped on a frog.

But who?

The odor grew overpowering as four pairs of eyes (if you don't count

Eenie whose name in elementary school was FourEyes because of

his glasses but if you do then it was five) began to water.

Still, no one said anything.

The odor was horrific, a delicate blend of sauerkraut burritos enrobed in swamp gas with a garnish of rotting flower vase water. If you have ever smelled a burning moldy pumpkin (and who among us hasn't?) you are on the right track to imagining this stench.

I am telling you, it was BAD. Someone HAD to say something. Or so one would think.

But let me tell you a little about our four professionals.

Eenie was an accountant at Flatt & U'Lance. He'd been there eleven years last May. His job was to account for every penny earned and every penny spent by every department, and he was good at it.

He was an expert, in fact, in keeping everyone else strictly accountable for his or her financial transactions both at work and at home, where he kept his wife on a strict budget which forced her to cut every imaginable corner *except* buying the store brand of peanut

butter. There was only one brand Eenie

would allow in the house and it better

be the extra super mega

crunchy style, let me tell you.

Eenie did love his midnight

snack of a spoonful of

peanut butter.   Or two.

But as for admitting

accountability for his

own actions – well,

that's another story.

He could skate out of a mortal sin, is what his friend said. For by the

time he'd explained the fiscal and fiduciary, factoring in the

foreseeable franchise fraud, his friend said, even Saint Peter would grow impatient and forget what Eenie was there for.

Even when he was just a lad, Eenie would get out of trouble by explaining what had happened and why and how in such tangled technical terms that his mom or his dad would invariably end up throwing their hands up in the air in resignation and saying, "Oh, never mind. Just don't do it again."

So he was for sure not going to admit responsibility for this environmental pollution.

Could we just hit 'pause' for a moment here? I don't want you to get the wrong idea about our

friend Eenie. In many ways he is a fine example
of a responsible member of society: he has never
been late for work; he has never been absent,
either, although Flatt & U'Lance has a generous
policy on paid personal holidays for their
employees. Eenie has never, however, taken
advantage of this opportunity even though his
accumulated hours are reabsorbed at the end of
each calendar year, so he does not even benefit
financially from his diligence.

And, also on the job, he is excruciatingly
responsible in the applications of the ideal
models of honest and ethical accounting
procedures. He is aware, always, that his
employer and, in fact, his entire profession can
be negatively affected by either shady dealings
or simple negligence. When he is at work, his

thoughts are focused strictly on the professional performance of his duties. So it isn't that he is a totally irresponsible person. It is just his sense of *personal* responsibility that could use a little tweaking.

Personal responsibility can best be defined as the ability to respond personally to mistakes. To admit one's individual participation in events that have either gone horribly wrong or have simply not gone as planned. To admit, in other words, that we have screwed up. But let me give you an example. Or three.

One day as she was driving in the country with her husband Joel and two kids whose names I can't recall, Gloria G's attention was captured by a particularly enticing yard sale on her left.   Not wanting to waste her or her family's time on a yard sale that looked worthwhile but turned out to be full of broken toys, stained t-shirts and those cheap glass vases that she already had plenty of under her own kitchen sink, Gloria drifted into the left lane to get a better look.

What she did not notice was that the slight rise in the road ahead was just high enough to block the view of any oncoming traffic. Not that anyone would be expecting any oncoming traffic that far out in the middle of nowhere. Unfortunately, however, there *was* oncoming traffic: a full-sized Dodge Ram driven by Good Old Bob S. and passengered by his dear wife of 37 years, Phylis whose name was supposed to be Phyllis but whose dad was too astonished that she was a Phyllis instead of the Phillip he'd expected that he misspelled her name on the forms for her birth certificate but then swore he'd meant to spell it 'differently' so her future teachers would not confuse her with any other Phyllis that might possibly be enrolled in the same classes.

Anyway, to avoid hitting Gloria head-on, Bob swerved into the lane she had just vacated. But Bob, first focusing on avoiding Gloria's vehicle, then noticed yet another vehicle behind where Gloria had just been. So, to avoid hitting that vehicle (which kept going after the accident, so we don't know that driver's name) Bob was forced off the road. And smack into the Chevy Citation that was parked off the road.

The Citation belonged to RaeAnn who had kindly driven her brother James out to the yard sale because he'd seen the ad in the local weekly paper that listed, among other items, a computer. Now, the fact that RaeAnn hadn't seen her brother in twenty years until he showed up on her doorstep having driven across country from California on a motorcycle with bald tires and so, therefore, had no way to transport said advertised computer back home again had nothing to do with Bob plowing into her Citation, so we won't even mention it here.

But what we will mention is Gloria's response to the accident: To the astonishment of all – Bob, Phylis, RaeAnn, James, and the two women who were holding the yard sale as a fund-raiser for the local food pantry, as well as the across-the-street neighbors who were yelling about it all being the fault of the yard sale holders – Gloria stepped out of her car and exclaimed, "This is all my fault. I was in the wrong lane at the wrong time. I take full responsibility."

Now just imagine that! Right in front of her kids! And her husband did not even tell her to shut up or to drop to the ground and flop like a chicken. He simply and calmly supported her in her admission of fault.

She apologized to Bob and Phylis and to RaeAnn who was especially dismayed as she had no collision coverage on her now squished Citation. Gloria requested of the yard sale holders that they call the police, and when the police

arrived an hour later (during which time the
yard sale women served all involved lemonade and
shortbread cookies while they chatted) Gloria
told the cops the same story: It was all her
fault.

But this example doesn't end here.   It seems
that Gloria's husband was being transferred in
less than two weeks, so she took it upon herself
to see that their insurance company covered the
damages to RaeAnn's vehicle.   Gloria even
called her at work the day before they moved to
make sure RaeAnn was satisfied with the repairs.

Now, we'll never know how Gloria was instilled
with her sense of responsibility, whether she
was raised that way or whether she chose it in

reaction against the way she was raised or whether it was some strange genetic combination of her DNA, but it is interesting to imagine what her two children would turn out like, being raised by such a mother.

Within this primary example of personal responsibility, are several secondary ones, and at least one tertiary one. Remember that Gloria, by being in the wrong lane, had in effect forced Bob into the path of an oncoming vehicle. Bob, in his turn, had to quickly make a decision. He could: 1)ram (no pun intended) into Gloria and her family, 2) ram into the oncoming vehicle, or 3) ram into the empty parked vehicle. Over the aforementioned lemonade and shortbread cookies, Bob explained his split-second decision: By ramming into the empty vehicle, he would harm only a *thing* (RaeAnn's Citation) and not a *person*. To him, there was no option. This was how Bob showed his personal responsibility.

RaeAnn also showed responsibility by being willing to drive her brother out to find a computer. By parking on the shoulder of the road instead of the driveway, she showed responsibility for being a crappy backer-outer (several dead mailboxes and a dented garage door could stand as evidence of this). She also showed responsibility when her brother was still sleeping on her sofa a month later, so she bought him two new tires for his motorcycle and a tank of gas, warning him of the predictions of an early and horrendous winter.

The women holding the yard sale also demonstrated a sense of responsibility, first by holding the ongoing yard sale to raise money for the local food bank. One of the women, Sarah, had once, during a particularly hard time after her divorce, been forced to rely on the kindness of strangers to feed her own kids. As humiliating as this was for her, when she got back on her feet, instead of erasing the painful memory of being deeply grateful for the dusty cans of lima beans and off-brand canned soups, Sarah committed herself to being one of the kind strangers willing to help others.

But, instead of simply cleaning out her pantry once a year and getting rid of unwanted foodstuffs, she and her best friend from elementary school, Patty, held a rummage sale for one month every summer to raise funds which they used, minus the cost of advertising of course, to purchase name-brand items to donate.

Patty and Sarah also volunteered to serve at the food pantry for one weekend a year so they could ensure that, for at least one weekend, people who came in for help would be treated with respect and dignity and not the snotty condescension Sarah had experienced.

We also have the example (albeit the negative example) of the people in the car who'd kept going although they'd witnessed the accident and could have had their perspectives included in the police report or offered aid had anyone been injured. I'm sure they had their reasons for not stopping. Let's just say their sense of responsibility was on 'mute' that day.

And finally we have the outraged neighbors,
offended by Sarah and Patty's annual yard sale.
Remember that they accused the yard sale of
being the cause of Gloria and Joel and Bob and
Phylis and RaeAnn and James' accident. As they
told the police officers who responded, "We knew
this was going to happen one day. These women
are a menace!"   And in this, they showed
responsibility by - oh, wait, no they didn't.
They, in fact, were so busy blaming all the
wrong people that even the cops shook their
heads and rolled their eyes.

Personal responsibility stands up and says,
without hesitation, "I did it." "It was all my
fault." "Blame me." Which might be easier to

do at the side of the road than in an elevator.
A reeking elevator at that.

Meenie was the office manager. No one was sure how long he'd been there because no one ever spoke to him of such intensely personal matters as his employment history. All they knew for sure was that he'd been there longer than anyone else. Some people even whispered that he'd been there long enough to be the one who'd pushed Old Man Lemming down the elevator shaft way back in'34, but of course that was just a kind of joke because that would make him nearly a hundred given that he would have been at least 20 years old when the old man died if he'd gone to office manager's college right after high school.

But everyone did believe the rumor that Meenie's own brother once said that saying Meenie was as mean as a snake was defamation – to snakes. Meenie was born blaming everyone else for everything and then making sure they were punished. Severely. He blamed the delivering doctor's forceps for his deviated septum (which was

actually true and actually a blessing as it prevented him from fully appreciating the effect of being simultaneously overly fond of dairy products and lactose intolerant).

Meenie blamed the army for his having to go to office manager's college. And he blamed the office manager's college for burning down and losing his transcript so he had to take a job working for his second cousin's third husband which limited his annual earning potential to roughly twice as much as the cost of the first house of the doctor who had caused his deviated septum.

So you can see, Meenie was surely not going to admit this social gaffe.

Our friend Meenie obviously has problems with personal responsibility.   But he doesn't necessarily see it that way.   Like Eenie, he is a diligent worker who never calls in sick unless he really is.   He takes care of his family's physical needs: food, clothing, and shelter. He pays his bills on time or earlier, most of the time.   He doesn't lie to anyone and doesn't ask anyone else to lie for him, either.   Not even on his tax returns.

On the job, he is every employer's ideal

employee: diligent, dependable, and dedicated.

So you see, Meenie is a responsible person. To

a point. But, there's more to personal

responsibility than close adherence to the rules

and regulations. Meenie doesn't get this. He

is not even aware that he is slacking in the

'personal' part of personal responsibility.

For Meenie is not into personal at all. He does

not know to care that other people don't like

him and don't trust him. Other people are of no

particular use to him beyond their roles in his

life.

His wife Margie, for example, has hopes and

dreams of her own that he is not aware of and so

cannot support if he wanted to. Or if he knew

how. And she has not told him of these hopes

and dreams because she knows only too well that
if he did, he would only disparage them. He
would scathingly 'explain' to her why she is not
smart enough or talented enough or educated
enough ever to succeed.   Besides, as Meenie has
told her many, many times, she is simply not
pretty enough.   For pretty, to Meenie's way of
thinking, is the only reason any woman is able
to succeed.   And indeed, he names the
successful pretty women of the world as examples
to support his belief.

Fortunately, Margie Meenie knows her husband is
full of shit.   She knows not only that there
are many, many successful women who are
perfectly plain *and* perfectly brilliant but also
that she is every bit as pretty as any woman
needs to be.   She also knows that she does not

need his support to succeed, does not need him at all, in fact. She knows that the truth is that *he* needs *her*.

Without her, he could not get through one hour of one day. Mrs. Meenie is perfectly aware that Mr. Meenie is the dependent one, and she considers his ignorance of this fact to be a handicap. His ignorance that human emotional needs are as vital as their physical or economic needs is a source of unending pity to her.

She feels so sorry for his emotional shortcoming that when her friends ask why she doesn't just leave him, she can only smile sadly and lift her shoulders. They think this means "I don't know," but it really means "Could you leave a

damaged puppy on the side of a busy highway?"
Like it or not, Margie is Meenie's wife, so
although loving him might look like a dirty job,
someone has to do it.

So, without Meenie's knowledge or support,
Margie pursues her dreams on her own.   And it
is very easy for her to do this as Meenie has
never once asked her what she did today, so she
never has to lie or to cover her tracks.   She
can keep her secret until she is ready to tell
him which will be very, very soon: her class in
barber college graduates this coming April.
And, as long as Margie expects nothing
supportive from him, she will not be
disappointed not to get it.   In this way, Margie
is exhibiting personal responsibility.

Expecting from others that which they have never shown themselves capable of giving is irresponsible. And unrealistic. Maybe even foolhardy.

Meenie is, for whatever reason, incapable of acknowledging the importance of healthy emotional relationships. Or any kind of emotional relationship, as a matter of fact. Human emotions, to him, signal a character flaw, a weakness. He laughs at people who are emotionally honest.

And Margie knows this. She has always known this. She knew this when she married him. Sometimes, when she has time to wonder about such things, she thinks maybe it was *why* she married him.

For Margie is, and always has been, emotionally sensitive, perhaps too sensitive. Our Margie is able not only to sense other people's feelings but to experience them as if they were her own. She is an empath and so can feel other people's pain or fear or joy or confusion which is no blessing, she would tell you. It can be exhausting.

Meenie's seeming total lack of empathy, his disregard of emotions has provided her with a perfect balance. If he had been more empathetic, more like her high school sweetheart, for example, they would have spent their whole married lives shoring up each other and the world. They might have six dogs and four cats, all rescues, of course, as her high school sweetheart actually does, and she would spend her whole life cleaning up after, feeding and watering, grooming and tending to the needs of every abandoned and unwanted and mistreated animal and child and adult in the whole county.

All of which, of course, is perfectly admirable, thinks Margie, but may be, just possibly could be, certainly might be personal responsibility gone amok. For sometimes, she thinks, being responsible for one's own actions is admirable, but being responsible for everyone else's may be something else.

If we continually clean up the messes made by someone else, aren't we, in effect, encouraging them to make more messes?

It is hard for her to visit their daughter
Lissa's dorm room at college, for example. It
is hard to see heaps of dirty clothes on the
floor and piles of books and papers and fast-
food bags and containers everywhere. It is hard
for her to breathe, too, as the room has an odd
moldy odor. It is hard for Margie to know that
others will judge her beautiful, smart, talented
daughter harshly because of her messiness. So
for the first year, Margie would clean up when
she visited.

She would take home dirty clothing and bring
back clean; she would bring garbage bags and
cleaning supplies; she would bring file folders
and desk organizers. And then, one day it
dawned on her that her daughter invited her to
visit so she'd clean for her. Her daughter was

using her as a maid service.

As hard as it was to see the mess her daughter chose to live in and as hard as it was to refuse to visit, Margie did. She did not visit her daughter until she was strong enough not to notice the mess. Not to clean up after Lissa. Not to impose her own standards on her daughter's space.

Now when she visits, Margie absolutely refuses to acknowledge any mess. She praises what she can and ignores the rest. She has returned her daughter's personal responsibility to her daughter, where it belongs. And, believe it or not, the last time she visited, Margie noticed the mess was less and the stench was greatly reduced.

Margie finally realized that personal
responsibility begins and ends with the person.
We are responsible for our own happiness, our
own satisfaction with life, our own dreams and
hopes and goals (which are hopes with wheels).
We are responsible for our own spaces, our own
places.   We are even responsible for our own
reactions to things others do or say.

But we are not responsible for those other
people's happiness, satisfaction, dreams, hopes,
goals, spaces, places, or what they say or do.

Others make their own decisions.   Parents and
spouses especially need to remember this.   No
one else is ever to blame for our actions, and
we are not to blame for theirs.
Meenie has it all wrong.

Poor Meenie.

Minee worked in data entry. He punched numbers all day and loved it. As his fingers played the keypad like a concertina, his imagination soared. All day long, all week, all month, and year after year, he punched numbers and lived a rich, full fantasy life. He traveled to foreign lands and alien planets and explored the depths of the oceans. He rescued damsels in distress and then had hot, steamy cups of tea with them.

Okay, okay, he was a little limited.   But a good person, basically. And for fun on his days off and in the evenings, he watched rented action-adventure movies on his ten-year-old combination tv-vcr in his tiny apartment with his three cats who were all rescues, of course.

Minee was an excruciatingly responsible person who wrote the checks for his bills a whole payday in advance and penciled their due dates on the envelopes in the upper right hand corners where the stamps would cover them, and then he'd slip them chronologically by that due date in a wire mesh organizer he bought at WalMart for $3.94 plus tax, of course, because it was a non-food item. He had his household chores scheduled on the kitchen wall calendar he'd

received free as a thank you for donating $10 to the National Society for the Prevention of Cruelty to Animals.

For example, each Monday he scoured his kitchen sink; each Tuesday he vacuumed; each Sunday afternoon he cooked up a pot of chili or bean soup (his Mom's secret recipe for Five Bean Blaster was his favorite) or whatever, which was easy to reheat after work

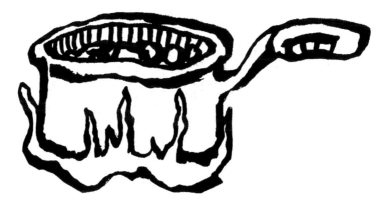

during the week. On the first Wednesday of each month, he called his mother in Duluth (after the rates went down, of course), and so on.

Minee was also exceedingly shy. Other than his mother on the first
Wednesday of each month after the rates went down, he had not
spoken (voluntarily) to a woman since high school when Wendy
Schneeburger had laughed in his poor hopeful but acne-bespotted
face when he'd asked her to the Homecoming dance. It had taken
him six years to work up the courage to speak to her at all, and her
ridicule was devastating. In fact, not only did he never (voluntarily)
speak to women, he barely spoke to other men either.

Minee was so painfully shy, even with his own family, that there was
a standing joke among them that if someone asked him a question
that he couldn't answer with a nod or a shake of his head, it would
take him seventeen days from Sunday to answer. This, of course,
was simply not true. But almost.

So you can see that there is no way that Minee could ever, *ever* possibly admit to this present atrocity.

Minee seems to be doing nothing wrong regarding personal responsibility, does he? He is a conscientious employee, son, citizen. He does everything he was raised to believe he is supposed to do. In fact, every moment of every day is driven by his mental 'Supposed To Do' list. But, unfortunately, he has left out a key ingredient of personal responsibility: happiness. There is no 'mine' in Minee's world.

We can tell that he is not truly happy by the nature of his daydreams. Minee has more in him than even he knows, and he is squandering his treasures in the pursuit of Supposed To. Clearly he has a frustrated sense of adventure.

And clearly he has a fantastic imagination. If only he could awaken those traits, he could live a more fulfilling, happier life. But how?

How is Minee to know there is more to life than 'Supposed to' when that is all he's known? You see, Minee's mom raised him and his sister Judee by herself since her husband decided it was more fun to secure a barstool down at Micky's Place from 10 a.m. to closing than to be a husband and father.

With no education beyond high school and no marketable skills beyond being a loving and responsible wife and mother, Minee's mom was hard pressed to support the three of them. But she did. And more. Minee's mom put an ad in the paper for cleaning people's houses and businesses.   She soon had all the work she could handle, but money is always an issue for a single mom, so Minee and Judee grew up watching their mother pinch every penny and cut every corner.

One night when he was supposed to be sound asleep, Minee got up to see why the kitchen light was still on.   He found his mother at the table with her checkbook and another book in front of her.   In the other book were several long columns of numbers.   When he asked his mom what she was doing, at first she was reluctant to tell him.   But then she shrugged and motioned for him to sit down.

Showing him the book full of numbers, she explained that when his dad left them, he also left a pile of bills. Dead Horses, she called them. Things he'd bought on credit but never paid off. One of them was her engagement ring. He'd insisted, against her wishes, that the ring she'd chosen needed a larger, grander stone. One that cost twice as much. He'd also bought a snow blower, and a canoe, and many other things they did not really need and that she had not wanted. He'd come back for the canoe and the snow blower, but she'd already sold the ring at ten cents on the dollar of its worth to feed the kids and keep a roof over their heads. Although the debts were in his name alone, she felt responsible for them and was paying them off a few dollars at a time. She told Minee that several of the creditors had told her to forget it, that they could write off the bad debts, but she refused. She was now in her eighth year, and two of the debts were almost paid off.

Minee never forgot that night. He fully understood the sacrifice his mother, and ultimately his sister and he, were making for his father's irresponsibility. On that night, Minee promised himself that he would always take care of his own responsibilities. And, although he was just a kid, he did. Always. No one ever had to ask him twice to take out the trash or to do his homework or to make his bed. He learned to cook by reading cookbooks and made sure that at the end of her hard day (and eventually night when she landed the Lemming Building cleaning job) she came home to a nourishing meal and a clean house. He also took on the responsibility of helping to raise

Judee who was as irresponsible as he was
responsible and who gave him and their mother
more than one headache.

Minee's mistake was in defining himself by what
his father was not. He did not ever fail to do
what he was supposed to, but he also never
allowed himself to explore any possibilities
beyond that foundation. He didn't need,
necessarily, to explore uncharted waters to find
the adventure he dreamed of. He might have
learned (and might yet learn) to stretch beyond
the basics.

A writing class at night at his local community
college might give him an outlet for his
creativity and imagination. Or he could learn
to think of his everyday routine as an

adventure, for many people do not have the
blessing, the sheer luxury of a humdrum
existence. He might force himself to make a
friend or two. Not that I'm implying it would
be easy to do, just tremendously worth it.

He might volunteer to help underprivileged kids
learn data entry, a skill they could actually
use. He might attend worship services and get
involved with a worthy cause or two. He might
very simply say hello to a stranger.

Minee has much to offer, but no sense of his own
worth. It may sound callous, but to allow the
thoughtless words and actions of a ne'er-do-well
father and a shallow, silly high school girl to
shape his self-image *is* irresponsible. He has
given to someone else what belongs solely to

him: the power to shape his life.

Who has not been ridiculed? Who has not been
rejected? Who has not been put down?   If we
all took to heart the thoughtlessness of others
as severely as Minee has, we would all be frozen
into the self-imposed deep freeze that he has.
Sheesh. The species would die out in no time.
What a waste.

Does Minee think that Wendy Schneeburger has
wasted a second in remorse or regret? Ha.
Wendy Schneeburger does not even remember him,
much less her own insensitivity.   And if he'd
attended the last three class reunions in
Duluth, he'd have seen for himself what has
become of Wendy Schneeburger: the same thing
that happens to all the Wendy Schneeburgers of

the world who regrettably peaked in the eleventh grade. Their long blond hair has thinned while they thickened. Her hourglass figure now is more of a figure eight which is fine if you are ice skating but not so fine for a person. Her inexpressibly sweet dimpled chin is now inexpressibly sweet dimpled chins. And her arches have fallen. Her clever one-liners have sharpened and become bitter and just plain nasty. Her third husband is an alcoholic oaf and her four kids are either in rehab or jail or should be.

Don't you just want to shake Minee? Wake up! Get a life. Have some fun. Break a rule or two. Laugh, for crying out loud. Thank the powers that be that Wendy Schneeburger was a snotty little bitch, Minee. Make eye contact

with your downstairs neighbor who is secretly
smitten with you but is too shy to make the
first move.   Marry her and have children and
raise them to be wonderful, responsible *and*
adventurous human beings.

Personal responsibility includes not only doing
what we are supposed to do, but also doing what
we might be able to do.   It includes trying.
Trying to grow, trying to succeed, trying to
learn, trying to live fully, trying to reach out
to others regardless of the possibility that
they will reject us, trying to make our own joy
and not waiting to trip
over it or slide
into it like
doggie
doodoo.

Moe, on the other hand, was a jovial sort. He was the accounts manager at Flatt & U'Lance and had, for quite a while, courted Madeleine Flatt, the daughter of *the* Flatt of Flatt & U'Lance and great-granddaughter of Old Dead Lemming. It hadn't worked out, of course, she being a lesbian and all, but they were still good friends. In fact, every Easter he supplied the ham for Easter dinner at Maddy and Patty's place to which it was understood he was

welcome to bring a date (and a pot of "his" Blue Ribbon baked

beans which he actually *bought – frequently* – at the deli and

dumped into a crock pot).

Moe had a way of making people who knew him only superficially

think he was just fabulous. He could remember their names for

years after only one meeting. He even knew their birth dates

(especially if they were clients) and had established the tradition of

sending a birthday card to each family member of each client

(current *and* prior as one never knows when a prior will become a

new current), each discreetly engraved with the firm's name and

logo (the birthday card, I mean, not the client).

He knew a joke for every occasion and could switch vernaculars and

levels of social and political correctness in a heartbeat. (He would

have made a great politician, in other words.) He always bought

the secretaries roses on
Secretary's Day but
always called them
Administrative
Assistants (the
secretaries,
not the roses). On
the surface, Moe was a
great guy. But
there was
one little flaw
in his character:
Moe had more excuses
than a dead deer has flies. I
swear, the man was
exasperating.

If he made a mistake, he'd admit it eventually, but first you'd have to listen to two thousand three hundred and forty-five excuses. Nothing was ever his fault. Nothing. Never. Never. Never.

So you can see that Moe was not fessin' up to the stench in that elevator.

Our pal Moe has no problem with people, he thinks. He is a true people person. He thinks. Unlike Minee, Moe is seldom alone. When his second wife left him, he already had a replacement primed to move in with him. As he wrote his wife letter after letter begging her to come home, he was doing the cashier at the grocery store and filing for divorce. When someone would ask why his wife left, he told one story after the other to cover up for the fact that he simply did not know. He had no clue why she would not want to be with him any more.

After all, he was such a fine fellow. He thought. But for Moe, being a fine fellow means being the life of the party, and the life of the party is fun at a party, but who would really want to live with that 24/7?   Moe does not understand that a forced jollity is not happiness.   A veneer of humor and thoughtfulness is not true thoughtfulness.

It is not thoughtful to flirt with other people especially in front of your spouse and then insist you are just "being friendly".   It is not thoughtful to buy her (or him) clothes you wish she would wear rather than something she would actually want.   It is not thoughtful to

trivialize her fears.   It is not thoughtful to
make a great show of being thoughtful, but never
really thinking of *her*.

It is not thoughtful to bring her roses when she
is allergic to them.   It is not thoughtful to
order her the drink your first wife preferred.
It is not thoughtful to make her scrambled eggs
with peppers and onions and grated potatoes and
hot sauce when she likes her eggs over easy and
plain.   And it is certainly not thoughtful to
call her by said first wife's name.   Most of
all, it is not thoughtful to deny you've done
these things when she tries to express her
feelings about them.

Moe did all of these things and more.   Worst of
all, Moe did not ever let her see his dark side

(which we all have) until well after the
wedding.   Althea, his second wife, was puzzled
when his cousin asked her if she'd yet met Mr.
Hyde.   She was confused when the same cousin
asked Moe how he'd gotten her to marry him. Was
she pregnant? Drunk?   She was perplexed when
Moe announced after their sixth anniversary that
now he "could relax".

As strange is it may seem, personal
responsibility also includes not defrauding the
people we claim to cherish. Althea had been
married before and had three children. After her
first date with Moe, her mother had asked, "You
didn't tell him about the kids, did you?"   This
appalled Althea. Of course she'd told him about
her kids. Why wouldn't she? "You'll scare him
off," her mother had warned, "No man wants a

woman with three kids."

Althea then promptly told Moe about every
mistake she'd ever made, every wrong turn, every
screw-up.   If he could be scared off, she
reasoned, he should be.   She lost her temper
with him, she swore at him, she stood him up.
She met him looking her absolute worst and then
some: no make-up, uncombed hair, and a faded
flannel shirt.

Then, of course, Moe asked Althea to marry him,
pulling from his pocket a handful of rings for
her to choose from.   The jeweler was a friend
of his and let him take them so she could select
her own.   At the time, Althea neglected to
notice that her selection had been pre-selected
and did not include a plain gold band as she'd

have preferred.

Moe chose the date, the time and place, the menu. Moe's sister chose the wedding cake, having just completed a course in cake decorating. Moe chose the honeymoon location which turned out to be a condo buy-in promotion and included a mandatory two-hour high pressure pitch.

Moe chose the restaurants they ate in and the music they listened to. Moe chose the friends they associated with and the church they attended. And eventually, Althea chose to leave.

But Moe never figured out why. To Moe, he was simply fulfilling his husbandly responsibilities

to take care of his "little wifey."
Unfortunately, Althea did not want to be taken
care of. She was perfectly capable of taking
care of herself and her kids and all of her own
responsibilities and she did not appreciate
being treated like a responsibility. Althea
wanted to be treated like a woman. Like a
person. Whenever she tried to explain this to
Moe, he would laugh at her. What on earth was
she talking about? Did she have any idea how
many women would be thrilled to be taken care
of?

Poor Moe. He probably truly loved Althea, but
he just could not understand the difference
between making a show of loving someone and
loving them, truly loving them. He could
simply not give up control of their

relationship, could not open his mind or heart as easily as he could his wallet.

Sometimes personal responsibility means allowing others theirs. Let me say that again: Sometimes personal responsibility means allowing others their own personal responsibility.

To Moe, it was inconceivable that Althea could be trusted to make such important decisions as where to eat and whom to associate with. He had met, fallen in love with, and married a strong, independent woman and then tried to treat her like a child.

But did he ever understand his mistake? Did he ever acknowledge his part in the failure of their marriage? Of course not. He told people that her parents had brainwashed her into leaving him, that she had a secret lover, that she was frigid, that she had never really loved him, that it was his idea that they split. And without a second thought, he promptly began to date again, this time a much younger woman. In fact, the same age as his daughter, this girl was delighted to be taken care of.

But wait. Althea is not without fault here, too. She, also shirked her personal responsibility. Remember how completely she made sure Moe knew what he was getting in the package called Althea? She knew it was important that he see her worst sides, not just the best ones. She hid nothing from him, so he could make his decision about her with all the cards on the table. But she forgot a whole half of the equation: *his* worst sides. She forgot to demand to see all of *his* cards.

Moe and Althea were married only six months after they began to date. Problem number one: Six months is not long enough to truly know anyone. Granted, sometimes a whole lifetime is not, and there are always exceptions. But in their case, it was certainly not.

We all have masks that we wear as the occasion dictates. False fronts we wear so people will like us or hire us or love us. But all masks are temporary. Keeping them up takes a tremendous amount of effort. It is exhausting. Eventually we relax and let our bare face, our true self, show. Althea knew this and worked against it, letting her true self show immediately.   But she had a further responsibility: to make sure she thoroughly knew Moe's before she agreed to marry him.

Unfortunately, it was easy for Moe to keep his mask up for six months because he wore it so much he often forgot it was a mask, confusing it for his true self.   If she had seen the worst side of him earlier, she could have saved them both a great deal of grief by breaking off their relationship sooner.

The bad news for Althea is that now she is afraid to trust her judgement about affairs of the heart.   She is afraid she will make the same mistake again and so avoids as much as *thinking* about another relationship.   In fact, whenever she sees any man who seems like a

jolly, happy fellow, she cringes.   Now she
assumes they are all full of shit, fake, phony,
lying, manipulative.

Again, we have an example of someone who has
become almost too responsible.   Like Minee,
Moe's wife has shifted from being a fully
responsible person to a person who is not aware
that she has another responsibility: creating a
joyous life.   For herself.   She has a
responsibility to examine what went wrong, to
analyze why it went wrong, and to make a viable
plan to avoid making the same mistake again.

Now, just let me say that Althea will
undoubtedly make other mistakes, many of them in
fact.   Althea is human, therefore she errs.
Growth does not mean learning not to make

mistakes; growth means not making the same
mistake over and over and over.

Now, obviously, all this background on our four professionals took
longer to tell than the trip up to the eighth floor and then back down
to the seventh. But I wanted you to understand the characters we're
dealing with. Actually, I'm not exactly sure how long that elevator
trip took because I wasn't really there that day, and yes I could, for
the sake of accurate reportage, hike myself down there with a
stopwatch and time it so I could include it for authenticity or
credibility or something, but I don't want to distract you with too

many details. So, let's get back on that elevator as it finally reached the eighth floor.

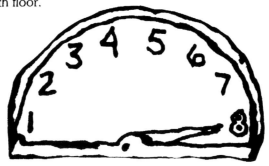

By this time, our four professionals were in truly agonizing olfactory distress, but nobody so far had said a word. They had wiped their eyes and pinched their noses (which never works anyway). They had squinted and squirmed; they had shuddered and shook. They had choked and gagged and very nearly sobbed out loud. Between the four of them, they had bit back a total of two hundred and seventy three inquiries and accusations and swallowed another seven dozen vocalizations of extreme discomfort and despair. They had twitched and tremored and tapped their toes in agonized impatience.

But they had not said one word.

At the eighth floor, the elevator stopped, and although ordinarily they would simply continue back down to the seventh, Eenie desperately clutched the control lever and threw open the door, praying for the slightest chance to dissipate the vile odor.

Unfortunately,

there was

someone

waiting for the

elevator. It was

Steve, the new copy boy.

Steve leaned

back and his eyes

got big and he

waved his hands in

front of his face and

he shouted,

"WHOOOEE.

WHO

CUT

THE CHEESE?"

Upon which, Eenie re-shut the door and pushed the seven button.

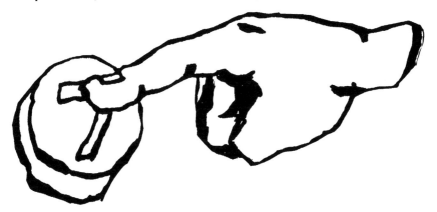

And no one said one stinking, lousy, apologetic, responsibility-

claiming word.

Did you think they would?   Sheesh.   Taking responsibility for our

actions is brave and decent and just generally the right thing to do.

But *come on* –

NO ONE IN THEIR RIGHT MIND ADMITS TO

FARTING IN AN ELEVATOR.

You too, owe it to yourself and to the world to find and then to do that special thing that no one else does in the exact same way that brings you fulfillment and joy. It is part of being personally responsible.

But wait. If that one thing that brings you joy is causing harm, loss, or havoc to others, please rethink the topic at hand: personal responsibility. Harming others is not a responsible act, even if you do accept responsibility afterward.

Have you ever seen those news clips where some felon or other is allowed at his sentencing to address the victim or the family of the victim? It seems appalling to me that they always say a variation on the same thing: "I'm sorry this had to happen to you/your family." Don't you sit there and scream at the TV, "It didn't *have* to happen, you cretin! You *made* it happen. It was not a random event! It was the direct effect of *your actions*!"

All the way across the social scale and back we can find examples of people trying to avoid responsibility for their actions. People outright lie or quibble or blame others all in an attempt to make themselves look better. Or feel better about themselves. In effect they are trying to save face, to retain their sense of pride or public image, but all they do is make every situation worse.

We humans tend to tolerate every human failing except arrogance. When our leaders or heroes or role models mess up, all they have to do is accept the responsibility for their actions. And apologize. And ask forgiveness. Instead of bare-faced lies and manipulations, bare faced contrition. Would work every time.

As well as these ways of looking at personal responsibility, there are plenty more. I'm sure you can think of some from your own life, your own experiences and observances. Some are in the negative, some in the positive. As we learn more from positive examples, let me call your attention to a form of personal responsibility that we often overlook: the responsibility to give positive reinforcement - - to *ourselves*.

Most of us know to positively reinforce desirable behavior in other people, but we often

forget to do the same for ourselves.   Think
about the things you've done well just in the
past week.   No, not necessarily life-saving,
world-shaking, soul-saving, spirit-lifting acts.
Just small everyday actions that you did well:

Did you defend an underdog?

Let someone else merge into traffic?

Resist the cutting remark to your mother-in-
law/ husband/wife/neighbor/co-
worker/sibling?

Handle a sticky situation with finesse?

Call a creditor before they had to call you?

Offer to help a stranded motorist?

Make the bed?

Shower thoroughly?

Floss?

Sure you did. Did you then give yourself your

props? I'm not talking about a tickertape parade every time you sneeze into a facial tissue instead of the computer screen. Just a bit of praise for yourself? Most of us forget to do this.

But think: If you would praise someone else for the same behavior, if you would thank them for their thoughtfulness or concern, if you would give them a quick smile or approving nod or a high five, why not do so for yourself?

When we congratulate others on their accomplishments, we reinforce their senses of worth and value. Doing unto others as we would have them do unto us is the foundation of positive human interactions. But why stop there? Why not also do unto *ourselves* as we would have others do unto us?

Some years ago, I read the advice: "Treat family as friends and friends as family." In any direction we might look, we can see people treating their friends better than they treat their own families, saying and doing things to their offspring, siblings, and parents that they would never dream of saying or doing to their friends. As if friends were precious, but family is dispensable.

I am not saying it is our personal responsibility to single-handedly mend decades-old family feuds. But we can handle our own part in the feud dynamic differently. Here are some examples:

Suzanne's oldest brother has recently insulted her for the last time.   She has ritually shredded and burnt his inflammatory letter to release the pain it caused her.

Their mother is dismayed and pleads for Suzanne to forgive him. "I hate to see my family at odds with each other."   Suzanne is tired of being the one expected always to forgive, to make overtures of reconciliation, to make emends. But she is also tired of trying to make her mother understand her feelings.   So, instead of getting defensive as she usually does, Suzanne instead calmly asks, "Mom, whatever happened between Aunt Jackie and you to cause the split in your relationship?"

Halfway through the explanation, her mother gets

it: Suzanne and her brother are repeating a traditional family dance that she herself has taught them. And, because she has learned to do so – finally, finally – Suzanne takes time to give herself the kudos she deserves for handling the situation responsibly.

Want another example? Okay, here's one: Max is sinking rapidly into an emotional black hole. He is aware enough to recognize the signs, and reaches out to his dad for advice.

"Tell me everything you think you're doing wrong," invites his dad.
So Max does, and the list is exhaustive: his work is taking him away from home more and more, his relationship with his wife is faltering, he misses spending time with his son and daughter,

his plans for home improvements has been forced onto God-only-knows-when-I'll-get-around-to-this status. And he's gained an uncomfortable amount of weight.

His dad waits patiently as Max's self-criticism unreels. When Max runs out of complaints about himself, his dad asks, "Now tell me what you have done right."

At first, Max is silent. The silence becomes uncomfortable, but his dad keeps waiting. Then his dad prompts, "Do you have bill collectors calling every day?"

"Heck no," says Max, "Adele is a great money manager. We're doing fine with our bills." "Okay," says his dad, "how are the kids?"

Max waxes eloquent with how smart and well-adjusted and happy his kids are, and how happy they are when he can be with them.

"What else?" asks his dad, "Is your job secure?"
"Heck yeah. I'm getting a promotion at the end of the month. A raise, too."
"Is everybody getting one?"
"No," says Max, starting to explain what had to happen for him to get this promotion. Then, Max gets it: there is much right about his life. He is doing a good job, the best job he can do under his current circumstances. He just forgot to appreciate his own best efforts. To allow himself some well-deserved pride of accomplishment.

Personal responsibility includes being

responsible for providing *for ourselves* the encouragement and appreciation we would reflexively offer to the people we care about. It also includes *becoming* one of these people we care about.

Would you like another example? No? No mas? Well, okay then. I guess you've got it.

It's time to go flex our newly-developed personal responsibility muscles. It is time to embrace every cliche we can think of regarding our personal responsibility: stepping up to the plate, eating crow, facing the music, and on and on and on.

No more "my parents were mean to me/other kids were mean to me/my husband or wife was mean to me."

No more "I didn't know it was wrong."

No more "I had too much sugar/alcohol//anger/
pharmaceuticals/bitterness in my system."

No more "I didn't get the pony/bicycle/video
game I wanted when I was four/eight/twelve."

What would the world look like if people simply
admitted their guilt and sincerely regretted
their actions?

What if people stopped blaming every- and anyone
else when they screw up?
What if all people took it upon themselves to
discover their true potential and then exert it?

What if even responsible people accepted that they are not responsible for anyone beyond themselves?

What if people were suddenly able to grant other people the right to be responsible for themselves?

What if people were suddenly able to give themselves credit for the things they do right?

Yeah, you're probably right: total chaos.

Never mind.